EDUCATED PARENTING

Copyright © 2019 by Kanika Blankenship
All rights reserved.

This book or any portion thereof may not be reproduced or used in any manner whatsoever without the express written permission of the publisher except for the use of brief quotations in a book review.

Printed in the United States of America

ISBN 978-0-578-44183-2

The Bright Idea Developers
P.O. Box 12854
Pensacola, FL 32591-2854

www.thebrightideadevelopers.com

Pictures/ Shutterstock Images

Cover Design by CC Milford
3 SIXTY Marketing Studio

For Nyala, Amiya, Miles, Blake, Baby Girl, and Michael

With all my love!

Table of Contents

Home Learning 1

Schooling 59

Activities 101

Behavior 121

Mental Health 153

Moving Forward 175

This book is for the parent(s) of:

_____

for the sole purpose of discovering the best practices of ensuring success in all aspects of their life.

Why Was This Guided Journal Developed?

I desire to reach all parents across cultural and social statuses. What we have in common is the love and well being we feel for our children. The need to be a well informed and productive parent is a universal goal. We have a desire to learn and use effective techniques that are best for the individualized success of our families. This book is merely a tool to help us all in our quest for optimal parenting.

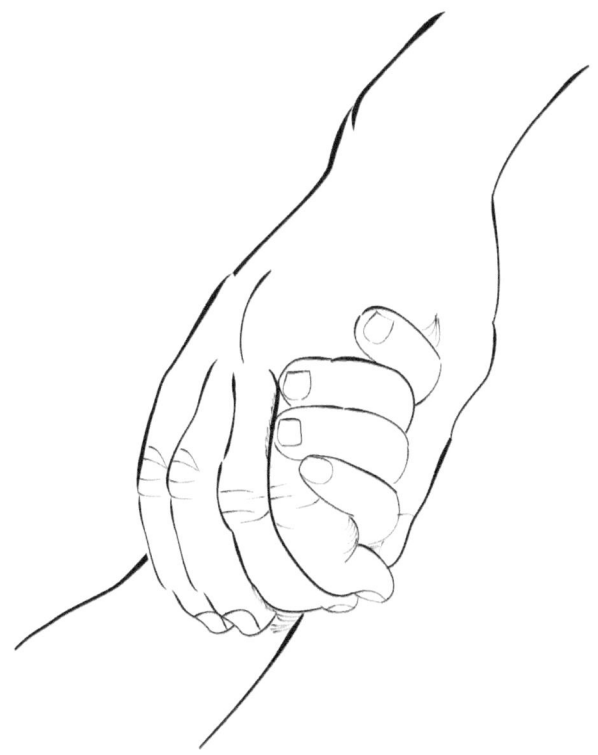

Who is Your Child?

From the time they were born, your child began to develop into a unique person. No one knows them better than you. If prompted, you could write a thesis paper concerning your child's morning and evening habits. For you, there are no surprises. You are fully aware of traits and nuances that develop the personality of your child.

When your child enters a classroom or any setting that involves an instructor, you should set the tone for the relationship between them and the educator. Establishing a good rapport and providing the teacher valuable information about your child is beneficial. Equipping the teacher(s) will give them basic knowledge that would help facilitate best practices when executing lessons in the classroom, assigning class duties, and grouping students according to academic level.

Take a good look at your child(ren) and write down all personality traits and what makes your child agreeable. I then want you to write mannerisms that make interactions with your child challenging. This inquiry is for you to have a better appreciation of who your child is. Acknowledging all personality traits will help with establishing effective communication.

Who Will You Assemble For Your Child's Team?

I can remember being a young mother and cultivating people in my life that would serve as co-teachers for my daughter. I had been fortunate enough to have been in fellowship with people from all walks of life, offering knowledge and time to the full support of my child. Both Immediate and extended family played the most valuable role in support. My husband and I could not have done this job, so successfully, without them. As for us, it honestly took a village.

Who will you enlist? The team you carefully recruit is not limited to family or friends. They may include health care professionals, community service organizers, and anyone in which your family comes in contact with and has a positive rapport. Feel free to share this "team roster" to better assist your child.

Sample Team Members

Psychologists

Au Pairs

Tutors

Dietitians

Dentists

Pediatricians

Coaches

Group Leaders

God Parents

Grand Parents

Dermatologists

The next five sections of this guided journal will help you take an inventory of your family practices at home, school, activities, behavior, and mental health. Maneuver in and out of these sections as you deem necessary. Re-visitations to challenging segments are highly encouraged.

Home Learning

> *You are the first teacher to your child. Spoken language, family culture, social norms, and basic etiquette are just a few subjects in which you develop an informal curriculum for your family.*
>
> — K. Blankenship

As a young mother over 21 years ago, I remember looking to the women in my family and peers for sound advice and practice on to how I should raise my child. I remember seeking the help of several parenting books and seminars to be successful in this new role that I was embarking.

I have since learned that although there are a plethora of tools available for us parents, there is no one-size-fit-all. I also learned that each family has their own value system. In my home, I chose to set a high value on education and the necessary tools to function into society. It was important to me to model these values for her.

My peers, who are mothers, had the same mentality. Our children were different in personality and interests, but together we shared a standard recipe in shaping our children. We looked at the individualized strengths, weaknesses, interests, and habits of our children, and created a unique experience in our homes for them to thrive and grow.

Look closely at your family and evaluate your current home ambiance and brainstorm ideas to make improvements.

What are your family values?

What practices are shared in your peer circle concerning child rearing?

I took a page from my parents with my own family. The way they reared me had left me with a clear sense of value for not only myself but for people around me.

As a military dependant, I've seen cultures of the world that some of my peers only read about in books. Being naturally gifted in Language Arts, I spent the majority of my downtime at home reading novels and writing poetry and short stories.

My most active times with my family were in the local culture of the people who lived around us. The countless festivals and neighborhood gatherings fostered my sense of appreciation for the different ways people experience our world.

I am thankful that most of that curiosity of life resides in my soul. I do everything I can to foster that same spirit into my daughter.

What lessons have you learned from your parents that you incorporate into your own family?

What life experiences would you like to facilitate in your family?

If it makes sense to say, my daughter is nothing like me but is precisely the way I was as a young woman. She knows what she wants and will not waste her time on tasks that do not interest her. She had discovered for herself, during adolescent development, that time is precious and should be spent doing things of value.

I had to be careful not to develop a "mini-me". Although I did expose a lot of things to my daughter in the home culturally, I had to listen to her needs and desires to make it a complete learning affair.

I must say I am pleased with the young lady that she has become. It is due to her platform. I trust her to continue to make the decisions that would help benefit her life.

What natural abilities does your child(ren) posses?

How do you and your child(ren) differ?

How are you similar?

I believe that we have the best intentions to pave the path ready for our children to thrive in the homes we prepare. I often refer to these walls of safety as "The Lab", since our children are affected by the environment we provide.

What dreams do you have for your child(ren)?

What is the contribution each person gives in your home?

How does your home climate affect your child's self-awareness and esteem?

The most valuable thing that you can give to your child is yourself. We are the first source of security, love, and comfort. The time spent with them and how you make them feel is what they will remember for a lifetime. Society and culture can interfere with the desired time you would like to spend with your child.

As a mother, I regularly take the time to evaluate myself and the interactions I have with my daughter. I had to make a personal inventory on how we appeared. I can admit times of struggle and uncertainty. I understood for myself that it was better to restructure some things in my home, rather than allow the dysfunction to continue. My child's well being was at stake. Perfect parenting resides on television and the entertainment stage. We all encounter moments of struggle. It is within these moments that we learn to appreciate our triumphs.

Describe your family culture.

What is the daily interaction between you and your child(ren)?

Is there time carved out during the day that each of you talks about your experiences away from one another?

Describe the moments you spend with your child(ren) when you are teaching them something.

Print Rich Environment

Most parents are aware of the importance of reading. It is the basis of all knowledge and understanding in every subject from reading a story to answer questions in language arts to solving the word problems in math. Studies show that a child should read for thirty-minutes daily to improve reading fluency.

When you look around your home, what can your child pick up to read? For young readers in your home, are you modeling good reading behaviors? Remember, our children like to emulate what they see us doing.

Young Readers:
What is your child's picture book inventory?

Who reads to your child? How often?

What pre-writing activities does your child complete? How often?

Older Readers
Describe your child's home library.

Describe your child's reading habits.

List all magazines with high educational content you have in your home.

List all books with high educational content you have in your home.

How can you improve in the area of home learning?

Schooling

"**D**isclosing the full academic history of your child provides the opportunity for the school to teach them, from day one, adequately. Work with the school to ensure your child has the best learning environment."

– K. Blankenship

Basic Definition of Learning Styles

Visual: Information has to be in diagrams/charts

Audio: Information has to be in spoken form

Reader / Writer: Information has to be in word form

Kinesthetic: Information has to be touched/manipulated

How Does Your Child Learn?

As a child, I was an avid independent learner. The way I best understood taught curriculum was to go back and read it for myself. I later realized that I was a better reader/writer learner. I have to see the information for it to sink into my memory bank. My daughter is a kinesthetic learner. She excels in project-based learning.

If you were to analyze yourself, for those who have not already, you could make the same discovery. We, as adults, know what best way to receive new information to remain competitive at our job, business, or life in general.

What style of learning does your child seem to excel? This information may not only be useful in the classroom but may help at home as well. Educators and psychologists have researched this topic for decades. You can find results on both sides of the argument of teaching according to learning styles. Write your findings about your child on the following pages.

I dreamed about who and what my daughter would become as soon as I found out about her pending arrival. I had a ready map of which school she would attend, how she would interact with others in the world, and what difference she would make to our community.

After I spent a considerable amount time creating the best possible learning environment in my home, I felt it imperative to ensure the school we choose for our daughter was optimal in standard. This decision was as crucial as the selection of the person's I placed on her "team." As a parent, I felt I needed to know what type of research-based curriculum the school I chose administered.

When choosing a school for my child when she entered primary school, I went along with the culture set among my peers and family members who had school-aged children. Becoming an educator myself, I later changed my focus on to my child directly. I had to determine what best educational setting worked best for her educational needs. In my community, having comfortable choices of a private, charter, and public schools made the search difficult at times. I knew no school was perfect.

My goal was to ensure there were open lines of communication between the teachers and me, a healthy academic plan, and a strong sense of community on campus. I spent countless nights researching schools and temperament of school culture to find that exact fit.

Will the school you chose to enroll your child accommodate your child's needs? Think about this question seriously, as your child will spend the bulk of their day within the walls of its campus. Ideally, I believe that with communication, behavior management, and a clear road map in curriculum administration, every school can be suitable for every child to thrive optimally.

What are the credentials of the teachers at your child's school?

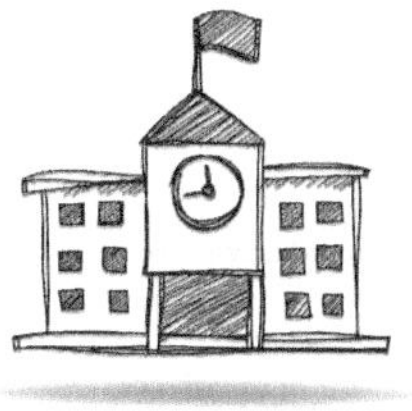

How does your school rate in the success of all students?

What is the culture of the school your chose?

You know the needs of your child. Every child requires some level of intervention to ensure they perform at an optimal academic level.

Some children crave for creative, independent assignments, a rubric for class curriculum, a seat in the front of the class, or require extra time on tests.

What are your child's academic needs?

What are your child's academic strengths?

I believe that knowing when to enlist help for your child is an important skill every parent should have.

My child required additional academic support that the school I chose did not offer. I added professionals from the private sector to add to the team I assembled for my child's success.

What type of academic support does your school of choice offer?

What professionals, in your community, will you need to help your child(ren) further academically?

Communication with teachers is paramount to the success of your child. What comes to my mind is the image of a small child coming home with a note pinned to their jacket, or shirt, to deliver to their parents. Communication has changed considerably since then. It is not uncommon to have standing parent/teacher conferences, video chats, e-mail, or telephone conversations at interval weeks.

How do you communicate with your child's teachers? How often?

Are you pleased with the level of communication between you, your child's teacher, and the school? How would you improve it?

Study Time

For academic success, study time is suggested to become incorporated in your child's daily routine. The intent, for scheduled study time at home, is to maximize daily learning and develop healthy study habits that go beyond your child's senior year in high school.

Which of your child's classes assign homework? Which ones do not? Are the learning expectations clear for your child(ren), and you, to understand?

Who helps your child(ren) with homework? Is the help consistent with your child's needs? Is there a set time for tutoring? How do you ensure the homework is done correctly and timely?

Are your child's book bag, study materials, and study space organized?
What is your organization routine?

How can your family improve in the area of schooling?

Activities

Our children shine in our eyes, in and out of the home. Keep them safe in everything they do.

— **K. Blankenship**

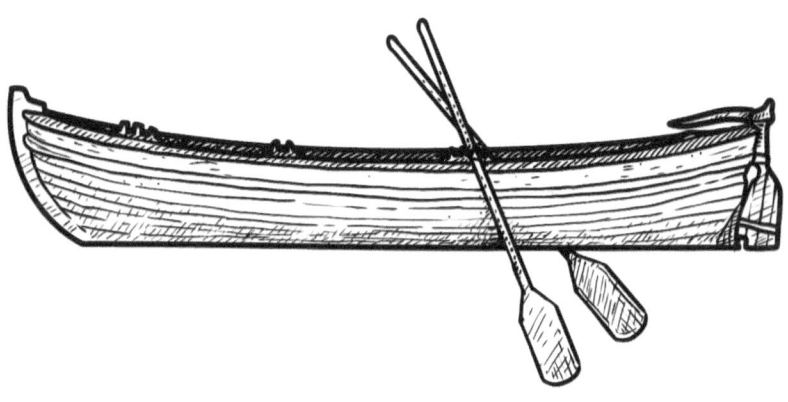

Every parent looks back on to their childhood and recalls positive experiences they participated in. My nostalgic walk down memory lane includes lessons in classical ballet and various other forms of dance lessons. In my neighborhood play sessions, I was a strong contender in kickball, short sprint racing, and monkey bar gymnastics. Riding bicycles and walking to meet up with other friends around our neighborhood was a daily activity. For me, it was never too hot or too cold to play outside. Being engaged with others doing some task was our definition of being active.

Our present-day children have a different view on the matter. Growing up with "New Age Technology" provides the children we are raising now with a different set of activities that just was not available to us as youngsters. Children are currently playing in virtual game leagues or are glued to their technology of choice to remain continuously active in cyber communities.

I feel it is our responsibility as parents to ensure that our children get the proper physical exercise needed to ensure optimal health. With any activity from gymnastics to contact football, there are reports of serious injury. I made myself aware of the risks. I attended every practice, game, performance, or meet to monitor my daughter.

What have been, and what currently are, your child's interests?

What physical activities are your child(ren) currently enrolled?

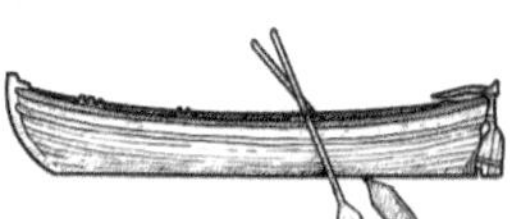

What performing arts classes are available in your city, that your child(ren) may have the interest to enroll?

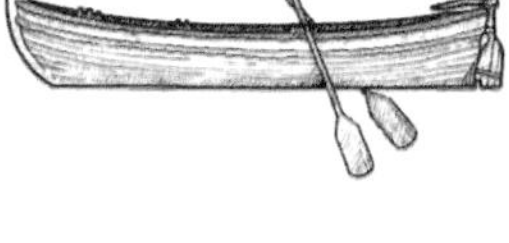

If your child(ren) is already involved in structured physical activity, or is involved in a non-structured physical activity, what steps are being taken to ensure your child's safety?

What non-profit organizations in your community have membership opportunities, activities, or seminars that your child(ren) can join?

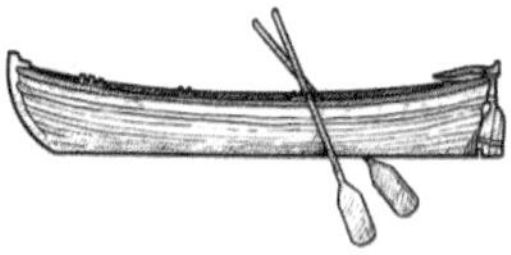

Exposure

We live in a multicultural society. No matter where I wanted to live and the people I chose to associate with, it was to my child's benefit if I exposed her to the many cultures this world has to offer. My optimal goal was to give my child first-hand experiences through travel. When I couldn't dash off to foreign lands, I made the most of the resources I had in my community.

When remembering my daughter's childhood, her interests changed as frequently as the weather. I believed it was my privilege to expose my child to everything positive that she found curious.

Aside from what I exposed my daughter to at home and school, my daughter got additional informal education from the activities she belonged. I have been a firm believer in engaging children into community events that foster a sense of community where they live. Every city has something to offer that is unique to their region.

What is your child(ren) culturally exposed to on a daily, weekly basis in your community?

How can your family improve in the area of activities?

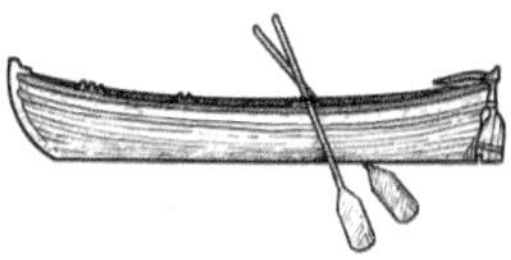

Behavior

"*How a child behaves in public is an indication on the culture and values expressed in the home.*"

— K. Blankenship

As a military dependent, formality was a social norm. Every aspect in the way we lived had a specific protocol. I knew how to speak, dress, and behave everywhere I went. Inside our home may have been a more relaxed environment, but boundaries were established. I understood that my parents were responsible for me and that their judgment, in matters, may supersede mine. I could talk to my parents about anything, and I also knew that it was not appropriate to speak to them offensively. As a parent, I adopted some of the same practices I learned as a child, and some I picked up along the way when raising my daughter. My husband and I developed a parenting style that was conducive for our household, keeping love at the forefront. Our goal was merely to raise a child that exemplified kindness, was respectful of them self, and demonstrate empathy for others in need.

What is your family's overall goal you actively work to achieve?

In some families, learning all forms of etiquette is essential. Is proper social interaction a vital skill taught in your family? What social values do you teach in your home?

What manners are unacceptable in your family? How is this behavior re-directed?

Learning how to treat people is ideally modeled at home. We all strive to have positive experiences, throughout our day, with people of both same and different cultures from our own. The family home is also the quintessential place to learn how to care for animals.

What lessons are you teaching your child(ren) on how to interact with people of authority?

What practices are being taught in your home concerning pets?

Have you met the families of your child's friends? Do they share your family / social values? Explain.

Do you have any concerns or issues with your child's friends? Have they been addressed?

Does your child(ren) have friends from different family backgrounds and cultures? Write about the diversity or non-diversity.

How does your child(ren) interact with other family members, peers, and all others in our society with varying exceptionalities? How accepting is your child(ren) to people that have differences from them?

Eating in public and private may look different in varied social settings. What should be the common thread in each situation is the comfort level of those around us as we share a meal.

Is dining etiquette being taught in your home? Describe your family meal practice.

Have you exposed your child to dining, formally and informally, outside of the home?
Describe your actions.

How can your family improve in the area of behavior?

Mental Health

"Caring for your child's mental health is as important as caring for their physical health."

— K. Blankenship

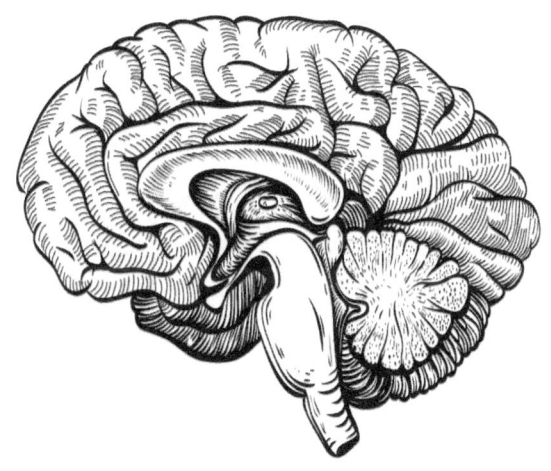

Understanding child behavior that is normal for each age group is helpful to parenting. In our society, we see many children who have experienced mental turmoil. Whether it is an effect of a tragic situation in the family, school bullying, peer pressure, or low self-esteem, some resources help combat these issues in our children's psyche. I have experience in battling mental health in children both personally and professionally. What I have learned in my experiences is to deal with issues promptly, honestly, and lovingly. We have to listen to the voice of our child. Ignoring mental health, emotional and psychological well-being, may lead to a situation that is far worse than the initial problem.

Taking an honest look at your child may take more time than you may have thought. Every child has a unique way of showing signs of mental stress that may not be as noticeable on the surface emotions they display. Remember, all forms of stress, whether a school assignment deadline to needing advice on peer relationships, warrants your attention. Stress can manifest itself to look like social withdrawal or self-mutilation. Confiding in your pediatrician will grant you additional resources of people who can help.

Do you feel that your child(ren) has a healthy self-esteem? What is your reasoning for this analysis?

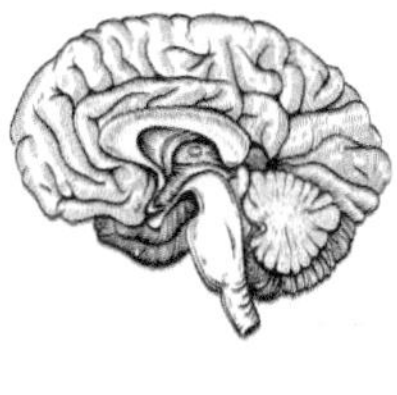

What type of general mood does your child(ren) exhibit daily?

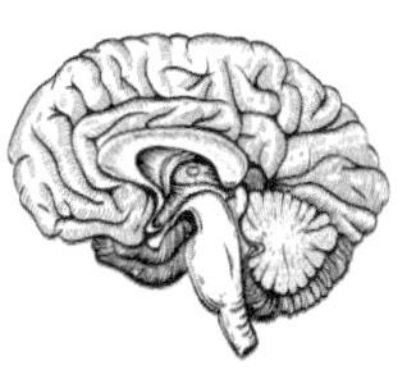

Has there been a sudden change in friends, physical appearance, eating habits, or spoken language? If so, what type of effect has this been on schoolwork, family/peer interaction, or extra-curricular activities?

_____

_____

_____

_____

_____

_____

_____

_____

_____

_____

_____

_____

_____

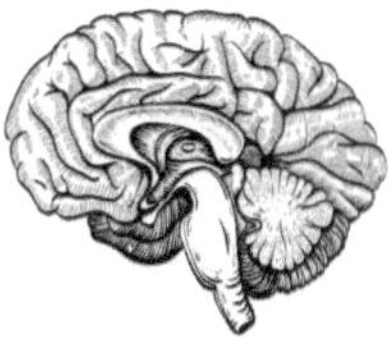

Do you suspect your child(ren) is hiding something from you? What evidence makes you feel this way? What is your plan to adequately address your concerns?

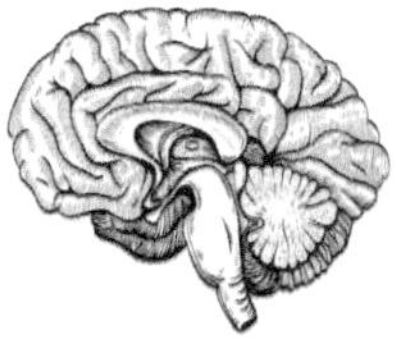

Who are the people in your community that can expertly assist you with the mental health of your child(ren)? Have you made contact? What is the plan of action to deal with the problem?

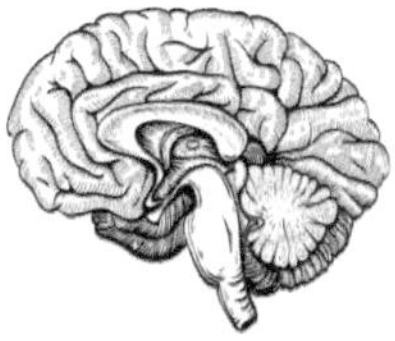

If your child(ren) is experiencing trauma from your home environment or community, what can you do to make a positive change?

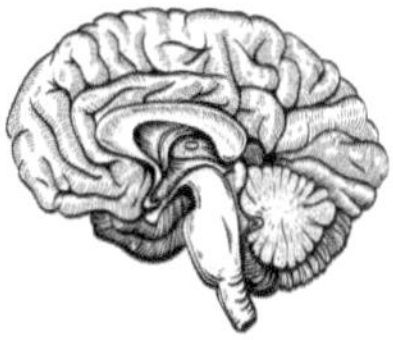

What is your reaction to your child's accepted or unaccepted behaviors?

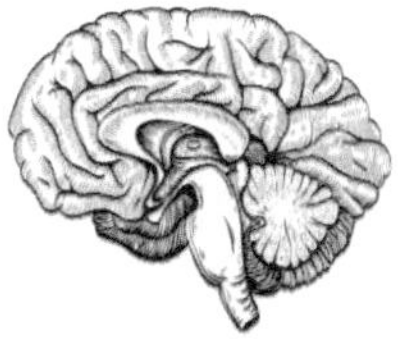

How does your response to your child's behavior affect your child?

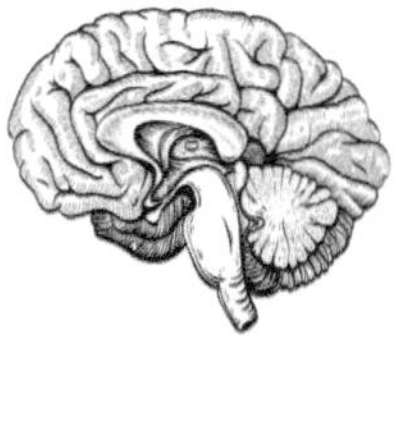

How can your family improve in the area of mental health?

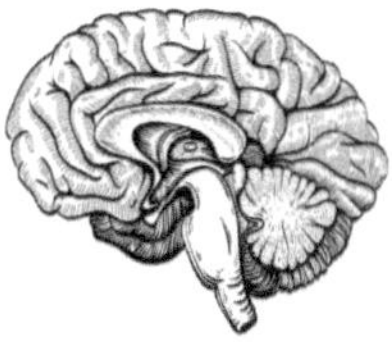

Moving Forward

"*Know when and where to share information concerning your child.*"

— K. Blankenship

As a parent, you have to determine how often you will evaluate the total health of your child. For general health maintenance, we visit our medical doctors yearly. Our contact increases when problems arise.

This Guided Journal helps to compartmentalize the many needs of your child(ren) and can be a treasured addition to your family.

Who do you plan to share this information with? What is your desired outcome?

Which section in this guided journal was the most difficult for you to complete? If it sparked uncomfortable feelings within you, what can you do to address those feelings effectively?

Your child(ren), no matter the circumstances, will always look to you for acceptance and love? What ways are you providing that level of comfort for them?

Describe how you are providing the best life for your child(ren)?

How can you improve in the area of moving forward?

I have often heard that parenting is the most rewarding, and most difficult, journey to experience in a lifetime. For me, I found this saying to be true. I am thankful to have had the pleasure of being someone's mother.

I wish for you the best of health and peace for your family. May your child be richly affected by your assessment of your household.

Thank you for allowing me to guide you on this journey.

K. Blankenship

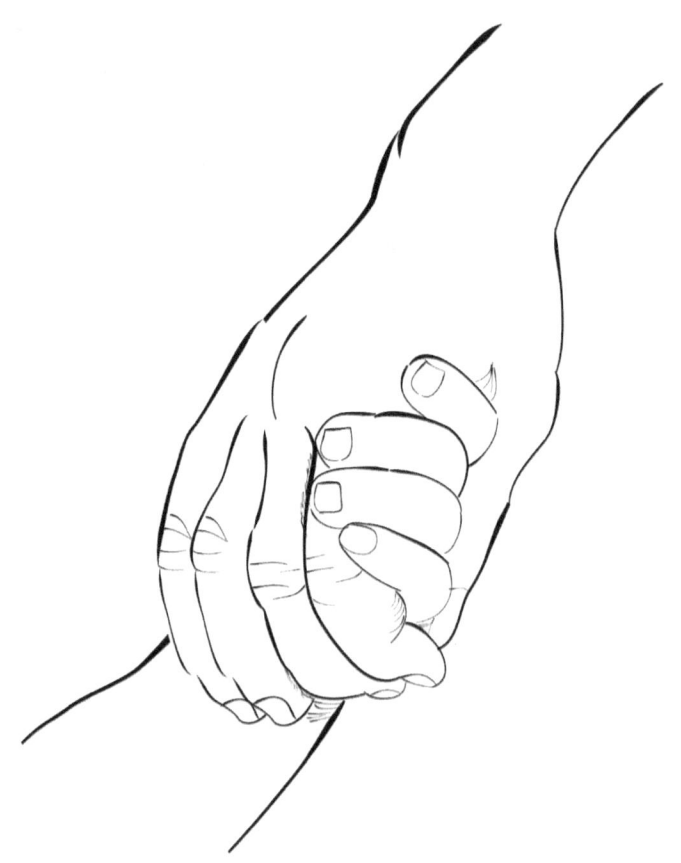

www.ingramcontent.com/pod-product-compliance
Lightning Source LLC
Chambersburg PA
CBHW021948290426
44108CB00012B/987